Sedition, Sorcery, and Blasphemy-Poems About America

Poet Ken Jones

"By culture, I mean the shared values of members of a society that are inculcated at an early age and pervade all aspects of living"

-Alan Greenspan, The Map and the Territory p. 225

"Americans have an amount of hypocrisy which is beyond any belief. Your humanity is a very selected humanity-only you suffer, only you feel"

-Zacarias Moussaoui-2006

Contents

AND NOW TO HONOR AMERICA...

The Native American Drum Circle
Chants "Genocide"

The Society for the Prevention of Cruelty to Animals
Growls "Shuffle off the Buffalo"

The Fraternal Order of the Knights of the Ku Klux Klan
Lynches "Dixie"

The Freedmen's Negro Band
Isn't allowed to sing

The Ballet de Folklorico de Mexico
Arrives with "Up Against the Wall, Mothers"

The Chinese Coolie Chorus
Grunts "I've Been Working on the Railroad"

The Mormon Tabernacle Choir
Reproduces "Seven Brides for One Brother"

The Vienna Sausages Boys Castrati
Trills hits from the musical
"Boystown starring Benjamin Franklin Nebraska"

The Congressional Barbershop Quartet
Harmonizes "We're Only in it for the Money"

The Temple Beth-El Cantors
Pray "This Land is Our Land, Too "

The U.S. Air Force Flying Tigers
Yodel The Muslim call to prayer

And we all sing as One
"We Shall Overcome"

AMERICAN PROCLAMATION

I emerge from 500 years of dominance:
Technological, Intellectual, Practical, Real.
Your concurrence is irrelevant. Live in my world's
White Shadow. Glowing over your possibilities
Girding your every reality
Glowering in the Power of our Selfish Society

I am the spawn of Human Conquerors
Who jerked the herd from tribal circles
To village Agriculture
To rapacious Industry
To Third Wave Cyber Society
Guided by the Enlightenment
Mill, Locke, Descartes,
Adam Smith and Thomas Jefferson
But denying the current dichotomy
Of PostModernism's decaying society
Is Insanity.

The same viral strain that brought Cristobal Colon
To a New World is either leading to New World Order
Or feeding on itself like a nationalist cannibal
Skunked by our Intersectional Junk
History is Bunk.

DEATH HEAD'S EMPIRE

Every empire day is another dollar down
Every earned night wears a spirit crown
Lost inside a corporate park we believe
Calm waste slips through it like a sieve
I've already lost more than most people ever own
I've already seen what most folks are never shown
White walled hallways amazed on Vegas TV
With many mansioned rooms of truth they let me see
We already have heaven's helping hand
Here in the blessed American land
But where we now go
Is a death head empire's blow
Instant epicenter of empty hipness
White wine flows like chilled piss
Hell is our long lost friend
Mystic Krewe, Sunshine's through, I make amends...

A NATIVE AMERICAN PRINCESS SPEAKS

All the elders know the change is coming. Mother Earth's been raped like I was when I was twelve. He entered my room when the Midnight Sun burned hot and high and stuck his tusk deep inside me like a dog sled pole in permafrost. In the village they make you keep the kid. I tried to be a good mother but the thought of it all made me angry. So I married a white man who worked on the military ships but his drill bit hit me again and soon three more babies joined the tribe. But I went nuts when he lied to me so they put me in the crazy house for six months and I just got out. So that's why I'm drinking in this stinking dive bar in the afternoon by myself. Wait! Don't touch me! You think you can tap on my shoulders to comfort me? Why don't you take your phony sympathy, wrap it in a quiet shawl and bowl your way back to whatever hell you crawled from-All I want is someone to trust and love.

OVERTHROW THE MILITARY INDUSTRIAL COMPLEX

"Chips of blank in boyish eyes"-Emily Dickinson

Somewhere an empire shakes in a spirit quake
Cleaves in two among those who claim they know
Original sin or past glory-a 230 year story
With chapters written both good and gory
Perhaps somewhere on the other side
Those who were ideals and pride
Can meet with arms open wide
To renew, replenish, abide...

PEACE RELEASE

An explosion of Old School
Scatters shards of this fool
Reconstituted into a new clock
Call me John Hancock

I'll sign first in line
For the revolutionary paradigm
The living pen a vibrant sign
Leave this growing, no win hatred behind

Seemingly futile, yet full of the pull
That transforms this dull word into a whole
Artifact of 21st Century attack
Once Enlightenment descends, there's no turning back

This vision stokes a fire of tolerance
A peace release in this desperate death dance

FROM AN AIRPLANE SEAT-AFTER WALT WHITMAN

Gray murky clouds pass my portal
As sunset's brightness ebbs and wanes
A red hot spot sandwiched between slices of sky.
Below, anonymous towns flank rivers
That snake through their bellies, the sandy dock sides
With curlicues of harbors, islets, coastlines,
White aspirin refineries, geometric houses,
The occasional pearly strand of electric lights
A peninsula under a river bridge, isolated islands,
The Hudson, East River, Manhattan
Denuded of Capital's phallusus
Three baseball diamonds
Like acid splotches of circular bandages
The flat maw of the river rippling lazily
The undulating carpet of clouds.

Somewhere a human remembers-this view was never part of
Whitman's mental camera-So when he asked what things would
look like a hundred years hence-wondering if the reader, the
sharer of the future, would see what he had seen, could he have
known his perspective itself would change perception? What a
question!

ARRIVAL-ECHO HOTEL

Eerie spirits sound around the Echo Hotel
Cocksure Kerouac rings a Road weary bell
Haunted Burroughs' wife-buckshot in her head
Open skull pours out a Naked Lunch of lead
Howling Allen Ginsburg in Vortex Sutra dread
Orlovsky passed out in the king size bed
Teetering on myriad invisible borders
Exploding boundaries between self and others
Let their righteous attitude
Fire our Texas Muses

THE NEW TROPICANA

Numerologists masturbate
In Vegas' empty face
The Vig-some mafioso's jizz
America's perfect paradise place
Where modern Roman numerals roll
Roulette backs in massive Craps
Poker with a Black Jack smack
Slot counters toll digital slaps
Disneyland for jaded wage slaves
Even has a Monorail!
Bearded transients beg for beer
Peasant immigrants come to fail
Or serve the bloated goats of Empire.
Women of a certain size
Hold their fat paws pinkies out
Their Spirit lack glows in their bovine eyes
As their men watch modern gladiator games
Boozing, betting, vetting rage
Draped in jerseys of their heroes
Displaying those devil numbers again.

Let me drive to the desert's edge
Hear the city's electric hum
Feel lonely isotopes destroy hope
Wait for the Apocalypse to come

WILL THIS BE ALL, SIR?

From the Hollywood Loews
I walked to the Pig
To whistle a warning
No one was listening.
Then to the Westin
My life steeped in sin
Again to a new morning
No one was listening.
I screamed at my comfort
My sick spirit hurt
So empty within
No one was listening.

MONSANTO OFF MAUI!

Mother Earth murderers
Off this Goddess paradise!
No! To your twisted genetic strands
Seeds of deception disguised as Life
Ali'i and Aina united against your lies
No! To your strains that stain the soil
To your defeat we raise our voices and fists
Off Maui forever until you cease to exist!

GROUNDHOG DAY-AUSTIN

A Texas Showdown on ancient Drags
Raul said he's bring the bag
But it all got greasy at Dirty's
Like the lost piss from a Lazy Daisy
So I took Junior to the Beach
Because Mother's was way out of reach
Sister Cindy was screaming in her cart
I returned to the Ark, but it was only worse.

The ancient Drag full of strange people
Who displace the natives from the East Side
Their speech and eyes so bland and dull
I was so far inside I felt outside
History caressed my marching feet
Rising like spirits in new Waterloo's streets

STAND BY ONE

Tans sprayed from bottle chemicals
Their creature comforts simple
Selfie smiles from hot young richies
Stiffen an old man's flaccid britches
Pearls like large light bulbs adorn
Thin pinched necks to the manor born
But I beg you, check your wrath and scorn
For man needs help from every creature born

SUBURBAN GANGS

I. Context of Greed

These stories sum up what youths in gangs want:
A sense of self-esteem and permanency
Plus some cash in their pockets.
Like in the inner city, criminal activity centers around
Physical assaults, the buying and selling
Of illegal substances, theft, and burglary.
The difference is that in affluent communities
Youths are not affected by economic blight
They simply rebel in a context of greed.

II. Mindset of the Offenders

To become a member, youths had to commit an outrageous
But not necessarily criminal act.
Two members, though, decided to burn down a "Port-a-Potty"
(An outdoor outhouse at their school).
This kind of "malicious mischief" doesn't qualify as gang activity
Especially because it was an isolated incident
However the mindset of the offenders was worth
Monitoring by local juvenile officials.

III.
In an affluent part of Lancaster, PA in 1992
The Beat Down Posse formed
The BDP took its name from the slang "beat down"
An expression used by youths
When they are going to assault and injure someone.

The Lancaster Youths, 10-14, most of whom came from broken homes
Threatened youth, assaulted others, and were caught shoplifting
Because they were young and law enforcement responded quickly
The gang was swiftly broken up.

HYPNOPHARMA

I'm a narcotized Narcissus
The TV is my pond
It's pharmacopoeia miracle cures
My medicinal magic wand
No wonder I can't sleep
Or face the next sunrise
I stare into the hypnoscreen
Drug commercials mesmerize
They sell you cures for ills
You never knew you had
Don't worry about the long term
Side effects can't be that bad
As long as Big Pharma
Reports enormous profits
And stock portfolios swell
In our system, all is well
So I sit back, numbly pacified
Another consumer on a zoned out ride

ALMOST A PSYCHOPATH

If you do the math
It's all about division
In our mental prison
Enjoy Your Wild America
As the Peasants stare at ya
Wait! You are a total loser
God is the ultimate chooser

WHY MANSON IS MY HERO

He dropped hits of acid

He started a cult

He lived in a commune in Cali

He banged hot hippies chicks
Then ordered them to murder

He landed a song on a Beach Boys album

He loved Paul McCartney's best song

He never personally killed anyone

BREAKDOWN ACROSTIC

Bubba, you be a long ways now from Texas
Rome ain't Houstin-Utica ain't Amarillo
Empires fall as oil fortunes rise
A gallon of gas pumped from an armadillo's shell
Kills Mother Earth who chokes on risk in the chapel
Distraught patriots resonate to the structure's pull
On her dying eyes I see reflections of my dollar bills
Wells push Texas crude as her holy tears spill
Now find the Breakdown here you Yankee Jacks and Jills

GAMBOLING GAMBLER (After Kenneth Koch)

It was good to lurk on a dock in Chicago
Overhead circled the cawing crow
Drowning in filthy bilge below
My next victim, screaming "No!"
I caught this Tyger by the toe
Slashed his sack with my stiletto
In a lost nut he went from full voiced soprano
To a whining, dying falsetto
I a fly swatter; he a mosquito
Both of us stars in this murderous fiasco
I hid his rigor mortis form among the cargo
Then went in triumph to the next casino

AVARICE

Though naked greed has a bad reputation
Here is a fact without disputation:
There is no freedom without money
No true summer days unless it's sunny
In the worship of objects are lost many souls
When things surround you they take their toll
The man in a mansion says "I'm not greedy"
But look at him from the view of the needy
You have what you need, then always crave more
You buy one thing now, next you go to the store
Until you stare forlornly at your bills
A world away from other real ills
One truth remains, no matter when you die
You can't take it with you, even if you try

ELECTORAL COLLEGE REVIEW

I had a front row seat in the gallery
Right in the eyes of the Xmas tree
On December 19th in the Texas State House
Not a shot was fired from an ancient bourse
The oil portraits of our ancestors
Bugmen with evolution's allure
To the blood of freedom's martyrs pure
Democracy began again to stir.
To a land of laws rules how citizens yearn
O Empire wide and glorious-time now to return
Individual rights in a republic of freedom
We prayed this day would finally come
Trip sent stopping mob rule?
A dumbed down empire of fools.
Words on parchment
Rules of order
A fattened larder
Harsh starch heaven sent
Though people die
The frame returns
Law inviolate followed to the end
Imperfect citizens weaving the best system
Possible among impossible diadems
Improbable because people aren't angels
All the eligible replacements are female
Electors can't be federal employees.

KINGSLAND FLOOD

People watching in the jury box
Everyone has a story
Some will end behind the locks
Others will walk free
Many need therapy

Sitting here behind the bar
Watching the public stare ahead
Some look down, some look afar
Others look asleep or dead
Many filled with dread

Everyday Fates decided
By the State and Corporations
I once despised and derided
Now stuck in this station
Pissed in this dissipating nation

CEASELESS FEELING

Afternoon sun bake away my ache
Warmed by its Lord's hard facts
Tanned by the hiding why you ask
Forgiven for future loser acts
You should have known better than that
Back here older you realize you're nothing
Was nothing before, some day nothing will be
Shot through with a ceaseless feeling
A will to live stolen, wanting healing
In the balls of Kansas grandfathers
Lie the seeds of a future famine

THE UGLY FACE OF COMMERCE

Everybody on the Internet
Thinks everyone else is a fool
Business strategy is broad
The consumer is a tool.
Individuals empowered
By their hollow dollars shout
If I build a great product
Patience will put it out
Truth is on the surface
Commerce wears an ugly face.

THE LIE

The Lie grew as it spread
Gathered inertia to its false core.

The Lie gave naive dreamers hope
The Lie grew so bold it interspersed itself
Into the fiber of every being it encountered

The Lie followed me everywhere I went

The Lie consumed my entire hard drive

The Lie, which I loved like a brother
Proved my undoing.

The Lie, galloping with a dollop of indifference
Served me well in any social situation

The Lie bought me a few more days of ingratitude

The Lie was a path to the Spirit I spent
My waking hours dismissing

The Lie washed its hands like Pontius Pilate

The Lie became the last friend I could trust

RACE AS A SOCIAL CONSTRUCT

Watch an innocent boy's face
As his mother debates
Others' uncontrolled hate
To keep him in his place

EVOLVED FEATURES

Follow where the line allows
Let the poem take you
Beyond meaning to somewhere
Only language goes
When freed of schemes to hoe
Row, Row, Roe v Wade
Twenty million aborted human eggs
Like caviar from a sturgeon
More cars for the surgeon
What difference Is Intersectionality
If Interconnectedness
Links all creatures
With Evolved features
Examine a bat's skeleton.
Fine bones like a human
Pig transplants so close
What about zoonoses?
Viral leaps flu these peeps
Kiss my coccyx, Creationists
I say fix the caviar shortage
By harvesting the eggs of the aborted

INTERSECTIONALITY BLUES

When "Subvert the Dominant Paradigm "
Becomes the Dominant Paradigm
Chaos inevitably
Pendulums to order
Reality asserts its hidden ace
Fear the consequence

ANIMUS HAS US

Tyrannical Father?
Benevolent Mother?
Mansplaining
Woman Gaining
Post Modern
Macho Muslims
Self-rotting culture
Vandal Vultures
Huns at the Gate
Society Pissipates
What once was great
Death March awaits
Versus Entrenched bias
Right and Wrong in a death dance
Seeking Yin/Yang balance

BOILED LOBSTER

Despite Neo-Marxist Post Modern
Intersectionality
Hierarchical Structures
Don't exist exclusively
In Capitalist society
Beware destroying the established Order
Chaos awaits beyond the border

KENSTRADAMUS QUATRAINS

The camel will dismantle an empire
Inimical to a truly now change
Bowing before the greatest power
This quaking land survives somehow

Voices over voids patrol cosmically
Placing controlled thoughts in empty minds
"We know why, but how is the question"
Bellicose rebels leave reason behind

WHITE PRIVILEGE (for Chris Carmona)

"Coyolxautiqui's song is only heard by dreamers, those who
inhabit the night and sign its songs" Chris Carmona

I live in giving midnight
Burn its tune into my spirit
I thrive in starkest darkness
Breaking star fire, seeking to spear it
Those who dwell in daylight's hell
Flee from me and fear it
My heart's lava too volcanic
For weak wilting flowers craving Sun's solace
This black night fever's all I've got
Though the foolish may take me for soulless
In truth I walk this dying planet
Great Spirit's desperate conduit
Gaia's final strangled cry
Torqued and morphed through my Third Eye
So as you forlornly ask "Why?"
I and I answers "Look to the sky"

SEDONA POEM

From 75 Red Rock Road
It's a short jaunt to the beauty of Sedona
From the 18th tee, the star scape gleams
On cool winter nights the calm home seems
Both oasis and base camp
Lit for travelers like a lighthouse lamp
Cathedral Rock from the porch with a cigar
Looks close enough to touch, and not too far
Down Verde Valley Road a vortex hike
Feeds magnetic energy the healing Earth likes,
To this place of special wonder, we offer our thanks
In Great Spirit's name on Oak Creek's banks

NEOTONY

(The retention of juvenile characteristics into adulthood)

Smashing mailboxes
Doing Nitrous Oxide hits
Drinking in the afternoon

Bashing poems out
Cranking stereos
Sleeping til noon

Where the loss is gross
And the gain is loss
And the lips are deserted
For a final gloss

I've retained
A life beyond the pain
For what gain?
To stop feeling insane
Rumbling thoughts in eyewheels caught
Secret scrambled hyper naughts
For these freedoms we fought
Disguised as alive trampled and sought

Once we settle into routine
We become nasty brutish and short

This is what life is
To the grownups

An endless series
Of wake ups and blow ups

Your apathy is staring
Empty eyed into distant space
Your destiny
Is trying to escape

Soon descended
Into confused pain
In the summer rain
Hot on my skin
But so cold within
Dropped on the tarmac
To never bounce back

TEEN-AGERS

Adults are dolts
With Frankenstein bolts
Working slaveries
In offices, fields, or factories
We are storm and stress
Listlessness
Rebelliousness
Adolescence is best
Before they chain our asses
In careers, fears, and classes

A NATIVE VILLAGE TOUR GUIDE SPEAKS

I'm 19 years old. What I just said was "welcome" in my native language. We had over a dozen dialects and each of these regions has their own forms and values. Some ate whale blubber-it's tasty but fattening! Some age moose, salmon, caribou, muskrats but not usually bears. The bears would try to eat us! Our houses were mostly driftwood. We didn't make ice homes- that was Canadian natives. We often entered through tunnels to keep the homes warm. Some cultures segregated the men and women into different dwellings. You know how young people can be-chasing boys makes me giggle even at my age. The leaders used to arrange marriages. Men were prized for hunting skills. Women for gatherings seeds now we are free to make our choices. The elders also taught us to respect all animals and our Earth. These totems teach the four poles of respect-for self, family, culture, and the environment.

But I'm afraid we're run out of time.

WHITE FENCES WAIT FOR TAINT

Nature crushes then she teaches
Preaches then absolves:
A purse snatched on an LA Street
By crack crazed canyon kids
A woman worn by weary years
Fights despite her fears
A wild-eyed child on Sid
Wields a blade at her face
"You'll be pushing up raises
Those drugs are making you crazy"
"Hey, shut the fuck up, Lady!"
One of the White Fences dances
To the jambox raps
A silhouette of a marionette
The strings hold his soul's sap.
To the Lady's lips he slips
The steel, then slashes at Chaos
Havoc, the wrecked
And wasted life where he's trapped
And sees in the lines of her eyes
And feels the steel striking harder
The Blood of the Martyrs
Firing his skin
And she didn't listen
To her husband's lesson:
Nature oppresses then sets us free.

TWELVE STRIKES

Midnight grabs my throat like a street punk slamming his Doc Martens into my esophagus. I lie awake on a mattress of sweat-the beads nails jabbing my skin, drawing warm dark blood which spreads across the black city sky-blank as my heart, starless as the ceiling of this jail-the drunk tank where I curdle uncomfortably like a neutered cat-the noise of iron doors-the cars rushing down slick streets-the clock ticking twelve bells of incarceration no intoxication can salve. This buzz may abate but tomorrow another midnight awaits.

TO FACEBOOK

Everyone's a narcissist
If you don't like me, I get pissed
Follow me on Facebook

Everyone needs new friends
If you don't your life soon ends
Follow me on Facebook

But don't get too close
The Empire's spy wears new clothes
Follow me on Facebook

All I can do now is look, look, look

Now you said something I don't like
I'll unfriend you like a tyke on a trike
Don't follow me on Facebook

Will you visit my listing wall
I bet it beats the bathroom stall
Don't follow me on Facebook

WHAT AN AD LITEM SHOULD LOOK FOR IN A TAX JUDGMENT (for Robert Cuevas)

You're either on the wheel or off the wheel
Mother Earth belongs to Great Spirit's Commonweal
Who spins the spokes at random
The impoverished lacking income
Might inherit land
Only the Great Mystery understands
The poor in currency
Might be rich in property
Is the holy ground, whether rarefied or humble
Subject to Caesar's angry grumble?
Shyster! Your pen mumbles
General denials and good faith defenses
Perhaps the best belief is tearing down the fences

NECESSARY PRIDE IN A WASTED LIFE

Peace on a dingy gray Santa Monica Beach
Morning clouds hang like dark pillow voids
Summer sunlight streams far out of reach
At the end of the country, no place left to go

Peer from the pier, P2P file sharing
Weary sunken eyes your face is wearing
Does the numbness mean you're though caring?
Can you survive such a wild pairing?

Will the waves rise so the surfers can pray
At the ocean's altar this chill Tuesday?
When will the Oppression finally clear away
So the spirits of Freedom can come out to play?

I like the vision of Los Angeles
From One World Way to Empire Avenue
Such unity is doubly blessed
A gift of manumission come from The New

Open the bars far and wide
There's no place you can possibly hide
Lose yourself in the Rebellion Tide
Let it take you for a shaking ride
Witness a nation of endless civil strife
Brutal systemic abuse rampant and rife
With necessary pride-glad to be alive
For this saving Change we strive

A DUNCE'S DANCE

Where the homeless cry on retread streets
To the land of empty gentry fading away
Where comfort once was your birthright
Now will you even survive the fight

Where loss is a daily mouthwash
Stinging like bling found and tossed
Where the distance is a dunce's dance
To a soft endemic spot disguised as a last chance

You think you can escape the deadly drill today
But all you have energy for is a place to pray
If Great Spirit really exists, let Him or Her pass
Upon me open head and brain, another worthless mass

BACK IN THE HAPPENING

Future? What future? We told ourselves when young
To the current led us to the banks we now lay on

A Cyberculture one click from Ecstasy
Or one crashed file from Entropy?
No matter. The Transcendent Spirit feels.

Eli Whitney , a Negro invented Interchangeable Parts.
Each human has a spirit worthy of dignity.
Treat each accordingly.

Spirit falls into a Found
One: Something from another world
A trance enchants
Wisdom walks a battered path
But busts up on the math.

He will wander far due to a troubled mind
Delivering a great people from oppression
Come in, Come in
Now, teach the children
Come in, Come in
Now teach the children

MICROAGRESSION HURTS

The bunting is out
Red, white and blue
The natives all shout
"Our hearts are still true"
But the bunt sign is on
It's a suicide squeeze
So the global elitists
Can wallow in ease
Our sky cries
In fierce microbursts
Floods from my eyes
MICROAGRESSION hurts
Globo-Homo Corporate Control
Psy-Op Mockingbird
Social Justice Warrior
Antifa Turd

BULGARIAN TAXI DRIVER IN LAS VE-GAS

America is a scam.
Communism is better.
The rich want you to think you can win
But they don't let you in.

CLUELESS BUNK

Random violence with racist overtones
The Gaslight mightily benefits
But responsible citizens know we've blown it
In concert with the Collision
The face that launched a thousand bricks
History is bunk and our society's sick

ORWELL WAS WRONG

Apathy is Liberating
Karma is Contagious
Wealth is a Superpower

AT MIDNIGHT NEW YEAR'S EVE TIMES SQUARE

Hell is a New Year with no Hope
All you ever loved is lost
Pissed away in dissipation
Popped like bad domestic sparkling whine
Your freedom dreams damaged and insane
No reason to even keep writing
Except it keeps the noose from tightening
Why do we live? Is there a point?
Or do you spend your life in vain
Except the moments you anoint
As respites from the pain
Repeat until death.